RAND M^cNALLY

DISCOVERY ATLAS OF NATIVE AMERICANS

Rand McNally for Kids™

Books•Maps•Atlases

Discovery Atlas of Native Americans

General manager: Russell L. Voisin
Managing editor: Jon M. Leverenz
Editor: Elizabeth Fagan Adelman
Production editor: Laura C. Schmidt
Manufacturing planner: Marianne Abraham

Discovery Atlas of Native Americans
Copyright © 1994 by Rand McNally & Company
Published and printed in the United States of America

Portions of this book were originally published in Rand McNally *Children's Atlas of Native Americans*, copyright © 1992 by Rand McNally.

Photograph credits
Arizona Office of Tourism: Page 50 Navajo. Francis Reddy: 8 Chichén Itzá. Mark Nohl, New Mexico Economic & Tourism Dept: 6 New Mexico. Milwaukee Public Museum: 9 Xochicalco; 17 Eskimo; 23 Kwakiutl; 30–31 Menominee; 39 Hidatsa; 53 Hopi; 54 Zapotec. National Museum of the American Indian, Smithsonian Institution: 20 Kutchin; 26 Massachuset; 27 Powhatan; 33 Seminole; 34 Creek; 46 Klamath; 55 Zapotec; 62–63 Mapuche. National Anthropological Archives, Smithsonian Institution: 31 Mohawk; 35 Cherokee; 41 Arapaho, Blackfoot; 44 Paiute, Shoshone; 45 Ute; 52–53 Apache; 62–63 Araucanian. Robert Frerck/Odyssey Prod. Chicago; 8 Teotihuacán; 10–11 Guatemala; 11 Mexico; 12 Machu Picchu; 13 Tambo Machay.

Rand McNally discovery atlas of Native Americans.
     p. cm.
    ''Rand McNally for kids.''
    Adaptation of: Rand McNally children's atlas of Native Americans.
    Includes index.
    ISBN 0-528-83678-1 (pbk.)
    1. Indians—Juvenile literature. 2. Indians—Maps for children.
[1. Indians. 2. Indians—Maps.] I. Rand McNally and Company.
II. Rand McNally children's atlas of Native Americans. III. Title: Discovery atlas of Native Americans.
E77.4.R36 1994   93-39472
                                        CIP
                                        AC

Contents

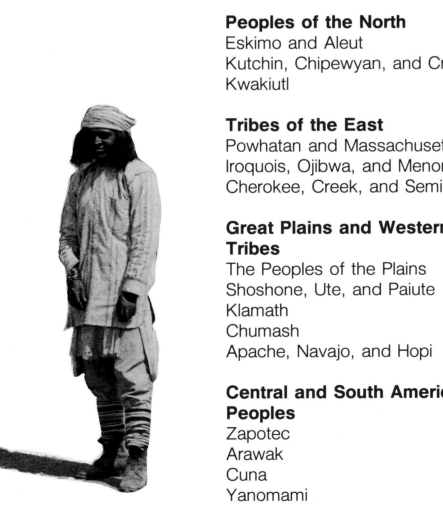

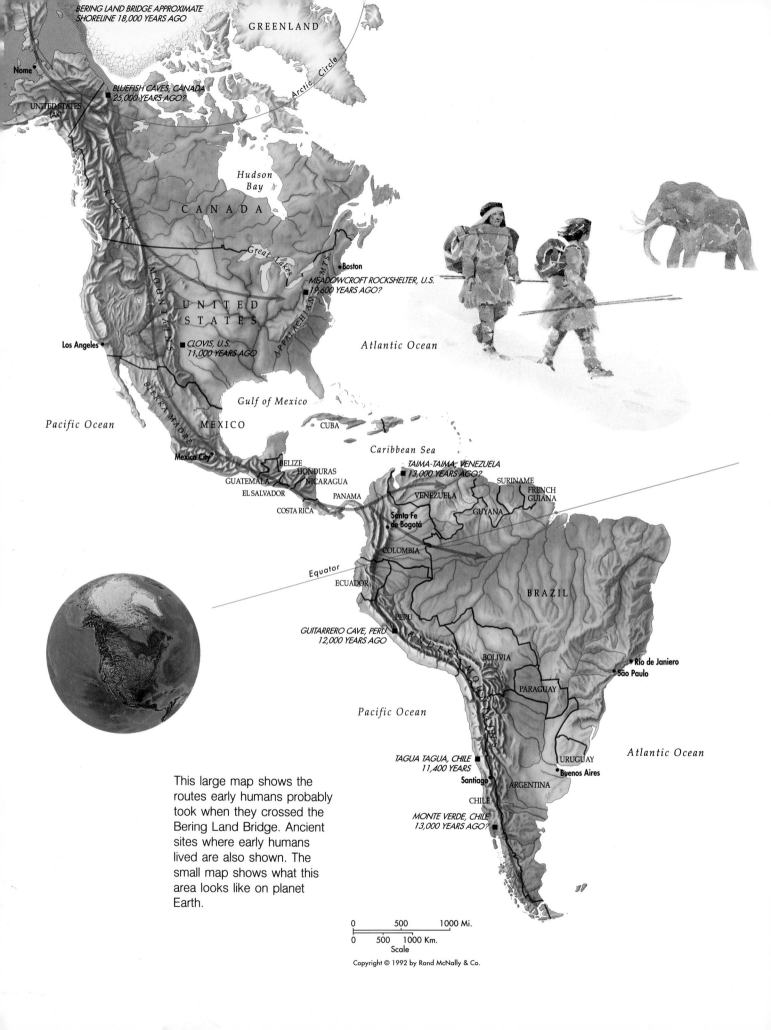

BERING LAND BRIDGE APPROXIMATE
SHORELINE 18,000 YEARS AGO

GREENLAND

Arctic Circle

Nome •

BLUEFISH CAVES, CANADA
25,000 YEARS AGO?

UNITED STATES
(AK)

Hudson
Bay

C A N A D A

Great Lakes

• Boston

MEADOWCROFT ROCKSHELTER, U.S.
19,600 YEARS AGO?

R O C K Y   M O U N T A I N S

U N I T E D
S T A T E S

A P P A L A C H I A N   M T S.

Los Angeles •

CLOVIS, U.S.
11,000 YEARS AGO

Atlantic Ocean

S I E R R A   M A D R E

Gulf of Mexico

Pacific Ocean

MEXICO

CUBA

Mexico City •

Caribbean Sea

BELIZE

TAIMA-TAIMA, VENEZUELA
13,000 YEARS AGO?

GUATEMALA
HONDURAS
NICARAGUA
EL SALVADOR

SURINAME

PANAMA

VENEZUELA

FRENCH
GUIANA

COSTA RICA

GUYANA

Santa Fe
de Bogotá

COLOMBIA

B R A Z I L

Equator

ECUADOR

A N D E S   M O U N T A I N S

PERU

GUITARRERO CAVE, PERÚ
12,000 YEARS AGO

BOLIVIA

• Rio de Janiero
• São Paulo

PARAGUAY

Pacific Ocean

TAGUA TAGUA, CHILE
11,400 YEARS

URUGUAY

Atlantic Ocean

Santiago •

• Buenos Aires

CHILE

ARGENTINA

MONTE VERDE, CHILE
13,000 YEARS AGO?

This large map shows the
routes early humans probably
took when they crossed the
Bering Land Bridge. Ancient
sites where early humans
lived are also shown. The
small map shows what this
area looks like on planet
Earth.

0   500   1000 Mi.

0   500   1000 Km.
Scale

Copyright © 1992 by Rand McNally & Co.

The First Americans

The Discovery of America

Long ago, there were no people at all in the Americas. Humans discovered America during the last Ice Age. Vast sheets of ice covered about one-third of Earth's surface. The ice locked away huge amounts of ocean water, so the sea level dropped by more than 300 feet. Where ocean waters now separate Asia and North America at the Bering Strait, a bridge of land was exposed. Between 30,000 and 50,000 years ago, small bands of Asians crossed this land bridge to become the first people in North America.

They came in waves of small groups over thousands of years. These first Americans probably followed herds of animals, which they depended on for food. By 20,000 BC, bands of hunters had spread throughout North America. Hundreds of generations later, by 10,000 BC, their descendants reached the tip of South America.

They lived in small groups in caves or simple wooden shelters. They used fire for cooking and protection and clothed themselves in animal hides and furs. For food, they hunted the animals of the vast grasslands and gathered seeds, berries, and roots.

Their tools were made of stone and bone. Spear points from this time can still be found throughout mainland United States, Alaska, southern Canada, and northern Mexico. They date from between 10,000 BC to 7000 BC.

During the last Ice Age, tribes followed animals across the land bridge between Asia and North America. The Americas were the last continents to be occupied by humans.

Bering Sea

The ruins of the cliff-side homes of the Rio Grande Anasazi can be seen at Bandelier National Monument, New Mexico. A group of Anasazi lived here from about AD 1400 to the late 1500s.

Cliff Dwellers and Mound Builders

Between 10,000 and 5,000 BC, the climate warmed. The vast glaciers and ice sheets melted from most of North America. The large animals that the early American Indians had hunted became extinct. The Indians trapped small animals, fished, and gathered plants to survive. By about 3500 BC, Indian groups that lived in what is now the southwestern United States had learned to farm. With a stable food supply, Native American cultures became more organized.

From about 300 BC to AD 1300, early desert groups shaped life in the Southwest. One of them was the Anasazi.

The Anasazi Indians built the first *pueblos*. These apartment-like buildings were placed on the tops of mesas. The Anasazi made them from sun-dried mud and straw bricks called *adobe*. After AD 1000, the Anasazi began building these pueblo villages on the ledges of cliffs where they were better protected against invaders.

These cliff-dwellers were excellent farmers, and their villages were large. Severe drought and invading tribes probably caused the Anasazi to break into smaller settlements around AD 1300.

Other early Indian cultures appeared in eastern and central North America: the Adena (100 BC to AD 200), the Hopewell (300 BC to AD 700) , and the Mississippian (AD 700 to 1500). They built tens of thousands of earth *mounds*. Most of the mounds were built in the Mississippi and Ohio river valleys. By the time of the Mississippian Indians, the mounds had become platforms for important buildings. The largest Mississippian village had one hundred burial and temple mounds and was home to tens of thousands of people.

GREENLAND

Arctic Circle

UNITED STATES (AK)

Yukon River

• Anchorage

Mackenzie River

Great Bear Lake

Great Slave Lake

Hudson Bay

C A N A D A

Lake Winnipeg

• Calgary

Great Lakes

Montréal •

Seattle •

Columbia River

R O C K Y   M O U N T A I N S

Missouri River

Mississippi

☉ AZTALAN, WI

Chicago •

New York •

Atlantic Ocean

CHILLICOTHE, OH ☐   ☐ MOUNDSVILLE, WV

Great Salt Lake

U N I T E D   S T A T E S

CAHOKIA, IL ☉

GREAT SERPENT MOUND, OH

A P P A L A C H I A N   M O U N T A I N S

San Francisco •

Ohio River

Colorado River

■ MESA VERDE, CO

This map shows the sites of some of the cliff-dwelling Anasazi ■, the mound-building Adena ☐, and Mississippian ☉ Indians. Many of these sites are open to visitors today.

CANYON DE CHELLY, AZ ■   ■ CHACO CANYON, NM

☉ ETOWAH, GA

Los Angeles •

SPIRO, OK ☉

OCMULGEE, GA ☉

Pacific Ocean

Dallas •

BELCHER, LA •

MOUNDVILLE, AL ☉

Rio Grande

S I E R R A   M A D R E

Miami •

Gulf of Mexico

M E X I C O

CUBA

Guadalajara •

Mexico City •

Caribbean Sea

BELIZE

HONDURAS

GUATEMALA

NICARAGUA

EL SALVADOR

| 0 | | 400 | | 800 Mi. |
| 0 | 400 | | 800 Km. | |

Scale

Copyright © 1992 by Rand McNally & Co.

The Great Civilizations

America's most advanced early civilizations rose to the south, in central and southern Mexico and along the west coast of South America. The earliest of these groups was the Maya. The Maya lived throughout what is now Guatemala, Honduras, Belize, and southern Mexico. After about 900 BC, the Maya began large-scale farming. They dug hundreds of miles of canals to carry water to and from their fields. Maya farmers grew enough food to support about two million people.

Between AD 1 and 150, people of the city of Teotihuacán built the enormous Pyramid of the Sun, shown here at the upper left.

A Mayan observatory, built around AD 900, stands in the heart of Chichén Itzá, Mexico. Later buildings, such as the pyramid in the background, show the influence of Toltec invaders.

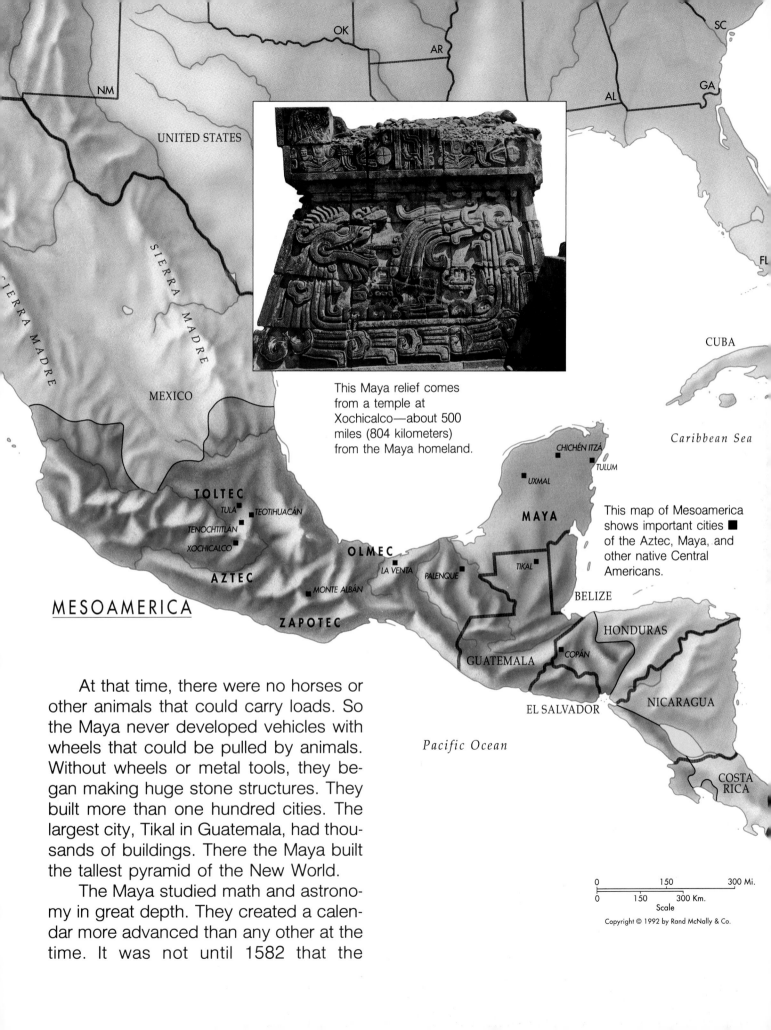

OK
AR
SC
NM
AL
GA

UNITED STATES

SIERRA MADRE

SIERRA MADRE

FL

MEXICO

CUBA

This Maya relief comes from a temple at Xochicalco—about 500 miles (804 kilometers) from the Maya homeland.

Caribbean Sea

CHICHÉN ITZÁ
TULUM
UXMAL

MAYA

This map of Mesoamerica shows important cities ■ of the Aztec, Maya, and other native Central Americans.

TOLTEC
TULA ■ ■ TEOTIHUACÁN
TENOCHTITLÁN ■
XOCHICALCO ■

OLMEC
LA VENTA ■
PALENQUE ■
TIKAL ■

AZTEC

MESOAMERICA

MONTE ALBÁN ■

BELIZE

ZAPOTEC

HONDURAS

GUATEMALA ■ COPÁN

EL SALVADOR

NICARAGUA

Pacific Ocean

COSTA RICA

At that time, there were no horses or other animals that could carry loads. So the Maya never developed vehicles with wheels that could be pulled by animals. Without wheels or metal tools, they began making huge stone structures. They built more than one hundred cities. The largest city, Tikal in Guatemala, had thousands of buildings. There the Maya built the tallest pyramid of the New World.

The Maya studied math and astronomy in great depth. They created a calendar more advanced than any other at the time. It was not until 1582 that the

0   150   300 Mi.
0   150   300 Km.
Scale

The Maya built the city of Tikal within a tropical forest in present-day Guatemala. The temples shown here were built around AD 700.

Europeans made a more accurate calendar. The Maya became the first New World group to keep written records using picture-writing, or *hieroglyphics*. Maya culture ended around AD 1200, although a few towns along the coasts survived for several hundred years more.

People calling themselves the *Mexicas* arrived in central Mexico around 1200. Because they had to compete with other groups for land, they built their first villages on land no one else wanted—the swampy islands in Lake Texcoco. We know these people as the Aztecs.

The Aztecs dug canals to drain the swamp. They created new farmland by making islands. The main village of Tenochtitlán grew on this new land. Canals connected its thousands of stone buildings. The city had parks, a zoo, and aqueducts that brought fresh water into the city from the mainland. The total number of people in Tenochtitlán was about 200,000, making it one of the world's largest cities at the time. Tenochtitlán stood where Mexico City stands today.

Like the Mayans and other groups of this area, the Aztecs used chocolate beans as a form of money. The ruling class drank a chocolate drink.

An Aztec temple, probably built between AD 1300 and 1470, is uncovered. The modern buildings of Mexico City tower in the background.

The warrior Toltecs were the most powerful people in Mexico between AD 900 and 1250. The ruins of their capital, Tula, are about 50 miles (80 kilometers) northwest of Mexico City.

Machu Picchu was probably the last Inca stronghold after the Spanish conquest of Peru in the 1500s. Its remains were not discovered until 1911.

Helped by neighboring cities, the people in Tenochtitlán ruled the Valley of Mexico by 1431. Then the Aztecs began taking over nearby villages to expand their empire. The Aztec Empire grew to include land from the Atlantic to the Pacific coasts. But it was held together by force, and the Indians of many cities were unhappy with Aztec rule. When Spanish explorer Hernán Cortés fought to take over the Aztec lands, these Indians helped his army. In 1521, Tenochtitlán and the Aztec Empire fell.

The Incas of South America developed the New World's most organized culture. Their lands included more area than any other group at the time. In AD 1100 they lived in the Cuzco valley of what is now Peru. After 1438 they used their powerful army to gain more land. Just before the arrival of Europeans, the Inca Empire stretched 2,500 miles (over 4,000 kilometers) along the Pacific coast of South America.

To connect this huge area, the Inca built 12,000 miles (19,000 kilometers) of roads. People and their llamas traveled these roads carrying goods to neighboring villages.

The Inca turned the steep slopes of the valleys into farmland by building terraces. They built huge stone buildings and created beautiful tapestries and pottery. The sun god was the main figure in Inca religion. The last Inca ruler, Huayna Capac, died in 1527. His sons fought for control and a long civil war began. The war ended in 1532, but the empire was weakened. When Francisco Pizarro led the Spanish conquest of Peru, the Inca Empire fell.

Caribbean Sea

VENEZUELA

Atlantic Ocean

GUYANA   SURINAME

COLOMBIA   FRENCH GUIANA

Equator

Quito

ECUADOR

River

Amazon

A
N
D
E
S

BRAZIL

PERU

Lima

Machu Picchu   Cuzco

Lake Titicaca   BOLIVIA

La Paz

M
O
U
N
T
A
I
N
S

Pacific Ocean

PARAGUAY

São Paulo   Rio de Janiero

0	300	600 Mi.
0	300	600 Km.

Scale

Copyright © 1992 by Rand McNally & Co.

CHILE   ARGENTINA   URUGUAY

Santiago

Buenos Aires

This map of South America shows the extent of the Inca Empire in the early 1500s.

An Inca girl today gets water from the irrigation stonework near Cuzco just as her ancestors did centuries ago.

GREENLAND

Bering
Sea

Nome

Aleutian
Islands

Arctic Circle

ARCTIC

UNITED STATES
(AK)

Yukon River

Anchorage

Mackenzie River

Great Bear
Lake

Great Slave Lake

Hudson
Bay

NORTHWEST
COAST

SUBARCTIC

C A N A D A

ROCKY

Calgary

Lake
Winnipeg

MOUNTAINS

Seattle

River

Columbia

Missouri River

Great

Lakes

Montréal

Mississippi

Chicago

New York

San Francisco

Great Salt
Lake

U N I T E D   S T A T E S

Colorado

River

Ohio

River

APPALACHIAN MOUNTAINS

Los Angeles

Pacific Ocean

Dallas

River

Atlantic
Ocean

SIERRA MADRE

Rio

Grande

Miami

Gulf of Mexico

CUBA

The large map shows the
northernmost culture regions
of North America. The small
map shows approximately
the same area on planet
Earth.

MEXICO

Guadalajara

Mexico City

BELIZE

HONDURAS

GUATEMALA

NICARAGUA

EL SALVADOR

Caribbean Se

0   400   800 Mi.

0   400   800 Km.

Scale

Copyright © 1992 by Rand McNally & Co.

Peoples of the North

Eskimo and Aleut

Some native groups live in the same area, sharing a similar language and way of life. The areas in which these groups live are sometimes called "culture areas." The Eskimo, or Inuit, and Aleut peoples live in the Arctic culture area, which extends across northern Alaska and Canada and even includes parts of northern Russia and Greenland. This is the largest culture area on earth. Ancestors of the Eskimo and Aleut reached North America much later than other Native Americans. They probably arrived by boat between 3000 and 1000 BC.

Eskimos call themselves "Inuit," which roughly means "the people" in English. "Eskimo" was the name given to these people by tribes to the south. The Inuit includes many groups of people who share the same ancestry and language. Long ago, they lived in all kinds of dwellings, including huts, hide tents, and *igloos*. The igloo was a temporary dwelling built from snow and blocks of ice. It was used only in the winter by the Canadian Inuit. In the summer they built tents out of driftwood and animal hides. The Inuit of Alaska and Greenland lived in more permanent box-shaped huts made from logs, whale ribs, stone, earth, and other materials.

The Arctic is a harsh land of snow and ice. Winters are long and cold and summers are short and cool. The ground itself stays frozen all year in a state called *permafrost*. Trees are unable to grow,

Armed with harpoons, Eskimo hunters prepare to strike at a large whale from their *umiak*. Made from driftwood and animal hides, these boats were up to 40 feet (12 meters) long.

This Aleut man wears a traditional hat carved from wood.

Aleut homes, called *barabaras* often held several families. A hole in the roof let smoke escape, but it also served as the door.

and only mosses, lichens, and a few flowering plants thrive. To survive in this region, Arctic people had to become skilled hunters.

Most Inuit groups lived along the shores of Hudson Bay and the Pacific, Arctic, and Atlantic Oceans. Fish and sea mammals such as seals, sea lions, walruses, and whales were important sources of food. Hunters glided silently through the water in one-person boats called *kayaks*. In a kayak, an Inuit could sneak up on prey to spear it. Much larger boats were used for whale hunting along the Alaskan coast.

The Inuit also hunted land mammals such as caribou, polar bears, and wolves. Some groups sped across the frozen landscape in sleds pulled by dogs. Other groups used snowshoes or spiked boots to make their way through the snow and ice.

The Aleut lived on the Alaskan peninsula and nearby islands. Their way of life was similar to that of the Inuit. They lived in houses made of driftwood, whale bone, and earth. Traveling in kayak-like boats, they traded both with the Inuit and the Indians of the Northwest.

ALEU

Aleutian Islands

Snow houses, or *igloos*, were built by certain Eskimo groups. These people used igloos only as temporary dwellings. Inside the igloo, families were crowded but they could stay remarkably warm.

SIBERIAN ESKIMO

NORTH ALASKAN ESKIMO

POLAR ESKIMO

GREENLAND

ARCTIC

Arctic Circle

BAFFIN ISLAND ESKIMO

GREENLAND ESKIMO

UNITED STATES (AK)

COPPER ESKIMO

CENTRAL ESKIMO

SOUTH ALASKAN ESKIMO

This map shows the Arctic culture area and identifies some of its major Native American groups.

LABRADOR ESKIMO

Hudson Bay

Pacific Ocean

ROCKY MOUNTAINS

CANADA
UNITED STATES

Great Lakes

Mississippi River

APPALACHIAN MOUNTAINS

New York

Chicago

0   400   800 Mi
0   200   400 Km.
Scale

Copyright © 1992 by Rand McNally & Co.

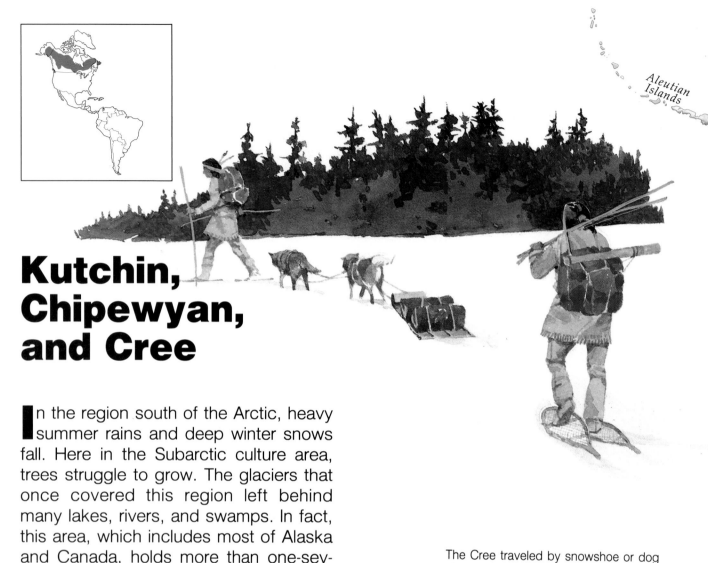

Aleutian Islands

Kutchin, Chipewyan, and Cree

In the region south of the Arctic, heavy summer rains and deep winter snows fall. Here in the Subarctic culture area, trees struggle to grow. The glaciers that once covered this region left behind many lakes, rivers, and swamps. In fact, this area, which includes most of Alaska and Canada, holds more than one-seventh of the world's fresh water.

Many American Indian groups lived in the Subarctic. Scholars divided them into two major groups based on the languages they spoke. West of Hudson Bay, groups including the Kutchin and Chipewyan spoke Athabascan. South and east of the bay, groups including the Cree spoke the Algonquian language.

The Cree traveled by snowshoe or dog sled in winter. Cree trappers traded their furs for French and English goods, such as beads, cloth, and guns.

GREENLAND

Arctic
Circle

UNITED STATES
(AK)

KOYUKON

TANAINA

KUTCHIN

TUTCHONE

YELLOWKNIFE

DOGRIB

KASKA

CHIPEWYAN

BEAVER

SUBARCTIC

Hudson
Bay

CARRIER

CREE

NASKAPI

CREE

CREE

MONTAGNAIS

BEOTHUK

ROCKY

OJIBWA

CANADA
UNITED STATES

Great

Lakes

Mississippi

MOUNTAINS

Chicago

• New York

River

APPALACHIAN MOUNTAINS

Los Angeles •

This map shows the
Subarctic culture area and
identifies some of its major
American Indian groups.

MEXICO

Atlantic Ocean

Gulf of Mexico

Pacific Ocean

0   400   800 Mi.

0   200   400 Km.

Scale

Copyright © 1992 by Rand McNally & Co.

The cold, damp climate and rocky soil of the subarctic made farming impossible, so the Indians were hunter-gatherers. They got most of their food either by hunting animals or by gathering plants. These Indians lived in small groups that moved often. They usually fished during the summer and hunted during the winter. Caribou provided an important source of food and clothing. Moose and mountain sheep were also hunted.

The Kutchin lived in the far northwest, on what is now the border of Alaska and Canada. Many Kutchin bands were influenced by the nearby Eskimos. For example, their birchbark canoes

These Kutchin children were photographed in Alaska in about 1926, after the Kutchin had given up many of their traditional ways.

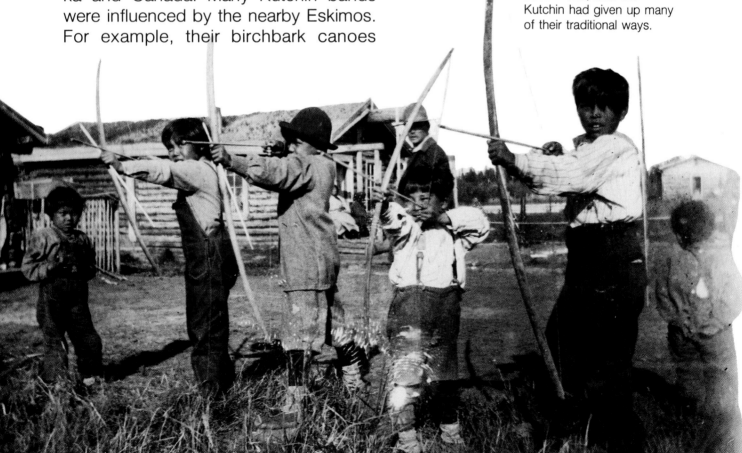

The caribou was a major resource for the Chipewyan. The animal hides were tanned to make tents or clothing, the bones were made into tools, and the meat fed the tribe.

were similar to the Eskimo umiak. The Kutchin used long, narrow snowshoes to trudge through the snow. They also traveled in Eskimo-style sleds. But their homes were more similar to the *tepees* made by the Plains Indians. These portable skin-tents were made from wooden frames covered with caribou hides. The Kutchin placed evergreen branches and hides on the frozen ground inside. Then they packed snow along the edges to keep out the cold.

The Chipewyans were the largest Native American group in northwestern Canada and Alaska. Caribou were very important to the Chipewyans. Caribou were hunted from canoes as they waded across rivers and snared with ropes on land. The Chipewyans used every part of the caribou. Its hide was used for clothes, laces, and tent coverings. Its bones and antlers became tools, and its meat fed the tribe.

Fish were another important source of food. There were many fish in the Subarctic waterways, and Chipewyans caught them any way they could. Fish were speared, hooked, or trapped in pens. Chipewyans also ate some of the few plants that grew in this harsh area, such as mosses and lichens.

The Cree were also hunters and trappers. They lived in cone-shaped tents covered with birch bark, or *wigwams*. The first groups lived near Hudson Bay. But in the late 1600s, the Cree began spreading through much of Canada. When European traders arrived in the 1600s, the Cree supplied them with animal furs, especially beaver fur.

One Cree group, called the Plains Cree, moved south into the plains. They lived in what is now Saskatchewan and Alberta in Canada. Their way of life was similar to the bison-hunting Plains Indians.

Kwakiutl

Warm ocean currents run along the coast from California to southern Alaska. The currents create warmer weather and heavy rainfall. Therefore, the groups that lived in this area had plenty of food from both land and sea.

Thick forests grow along this North-west Coast. The peoples that settled here became skilled woodworkers. They made huge *dugout canoes* by hollowing out redwood or cedar logs. They built large houses from red cedar with beautiful *totem poles* towering in front.

The Kwakiutl were known for the detailed wooden masks they carved. The masks were used in special ceremonies. The Kwakiutl shared many practices with other Northwest Coast tribes, including the *potlatch*. The purpose of a potlatch usually was to establish rank within a village. Those giving a potlatch provided a feast for their guests. Then they gave away or destroyed many of their belongings. Those who gave away the most were the highest in rank.

This is an exhibit showing a Kwakiutl Hamasta Ceremony. A new member enters a secret room where he is told about the group's spiritual ancestors. Here the new member is being helped out of the secret room.

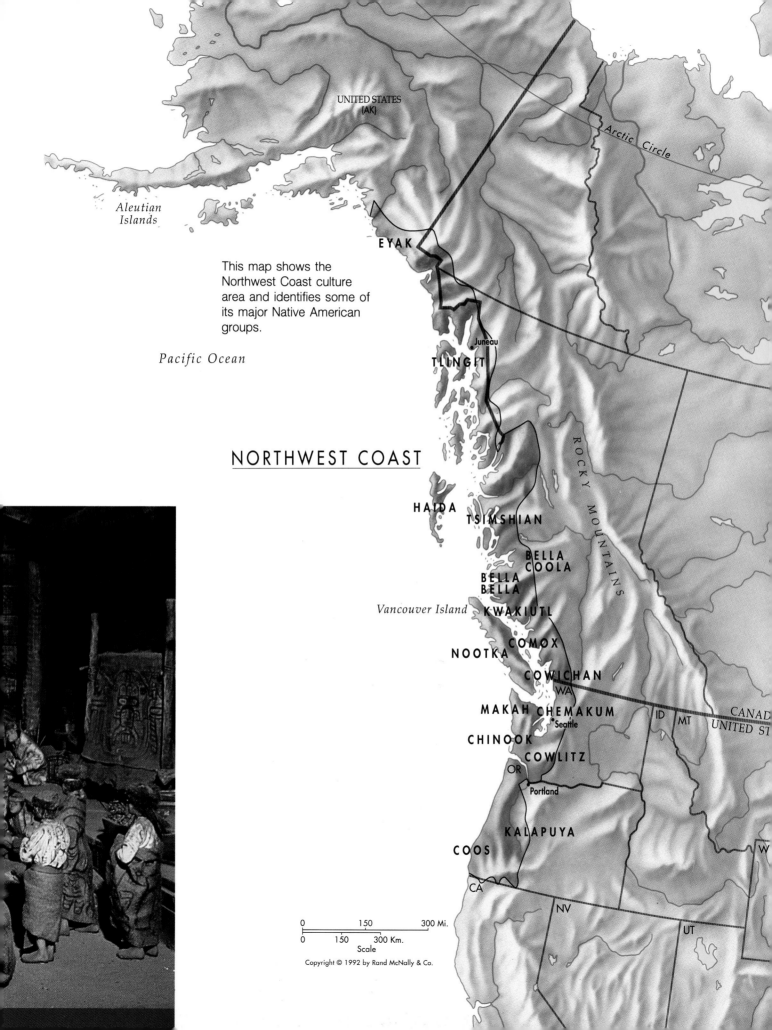

UNITED STATES
(AK)

*Aleutian
Islands*

This map shows the
Northwest Coast culture
area and identifies some of
its major Native American
groups.

Pacific Ocean

Arctic Circle

EYAK

•Juneau

TLINGIT

NORTHWEST COAST

HAIDA

TSIMSHIAN

BELLA
COOLA

BELLA
BELLA

Vancouver Island   KWAKIUTL

COMOX

NOOTKA

COWICHAN

WA

MAKAH CHEMAKUM

•Seattle

CHINOOK

COWLITZ

OR

•Portland

KALAPUYA

COOS

CA

NV

UT

R O C K Y   M O U N T A I N S

ID   MT

CANAD

UNITED ST

W

0   150   300 Mi.
0   150   300 Km.
Scale

Copyright © 1992 by Rand McNally & Co.

GREENLAND

*Bering
Sea*

Nome

Arctic Circle

Yukon River

UNITED STATES (AK)

Anchorage

Mackenzie River

*Great Bear
Lake*

Great Slave Lake

*Hudson
Bay*

C A N A D A

Pacific Ocean

Calgary

R O C K Y   M O U N T A I N S

*Lake
Winnipeg*

Seattle

River

Columbia

The large map shows the eastern culture areas of North America. The small map shows approximately the same area on planet Earth.

Missouri River

Great Lakes

Montréal

NORTHEAST

New York

Mississippi

Chicago

*Great Salt
Lake*

San Francisco

U N I T E D   S T A T E S

Ohio   *River*

A P P A L A C H I A N   M O U N T A I N S

Los Angeles

Colorado   *River*

Dallas

SOUTHEAST

Atlantic Ocean

River

Rio

Grande

S I E R R A   M A D R E

Miami

Gulf of Mexico

CUBA

MEXICO

Caribbean

Guadalajara

Mexico City

BELIZE

HONDURAS

GUATEMALA

NICARAGUA

EL SALVADOR

0	400	800 Mi.
0	400	800 Km.

Scale

Tribes of the East

Powhatan and Massachuset

The American Indians of the northeastern woodlands lived in permanent communities. The cold weather of the Northeast made farming difficult, but the woodlands provided a rich diet all year round.

These Native Americans collected sap from maple trees in the spring. Then they boiled off the water to make maple syrup. Berries, nuts, and roots were gathered later in the year. They fished in every season but winter. Hunting was best in the fall, and deer was the most important prey. American Indians along the Atlantic coast gathered shellfish. Those near the Great Lakes collected wild rice.

Native Americans of the Northeast lived in two types of homes: the *longhouse* and the wigwam. Longhouses were made of log frames and were sometimes over one hundred feet long. Wigwams were often dome-shaped. They were made of arched wooden poles covered with bark, reeds, or woven mats.

A Powhatan family works in front of a dwelling where many families live. The house is made of arched saplings covered with bark and woven mats. Tall, ripening corn grows nearby.

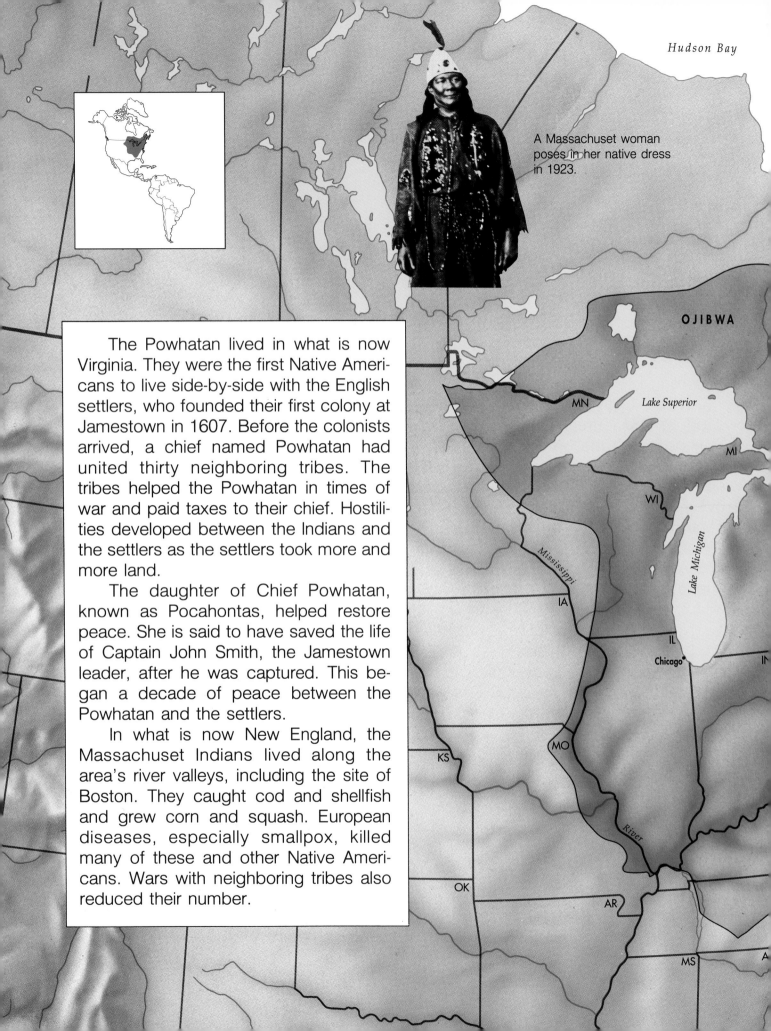

A Massachuset woman poses in her native dress in 1923.

OJIBWA

Lake Superior

MN

MI

WI

Lake Michigan

Mississippi

IA

IL

Chicago

IN

KS

MO

River

OK

AR

MS

A

The Powhatan lived in what is now Virginia. They were the first Native Americans to live side-by-side with the English settlers, who founded their first colony at Jamestown in 1607. Before the colonists arrived, a chief named Powhatan had united thirty neighboring tribes. The tribes helped the Powhatan in times of war and paid taxes to their chief. Hostilities developed between the Indians and the settlers as the settlers took more and more land.

The daughter of Chief Powhatan, known as Pocahontas, helped restore peace. She is said to have saved the life of Captain John Smith, the Jamestown leader, after he was captured. This began a decade of peace between the Powhatan and the settlers.

In what is now New England, the Massachuset Indians lived along the area's river valleys, including the site of Boston. They caught cod and shellfish and grew corn and squash. European diseases, especially smallpox, killed many of these and other Native Americans. Wars with neighboring tribes also reduced their number.

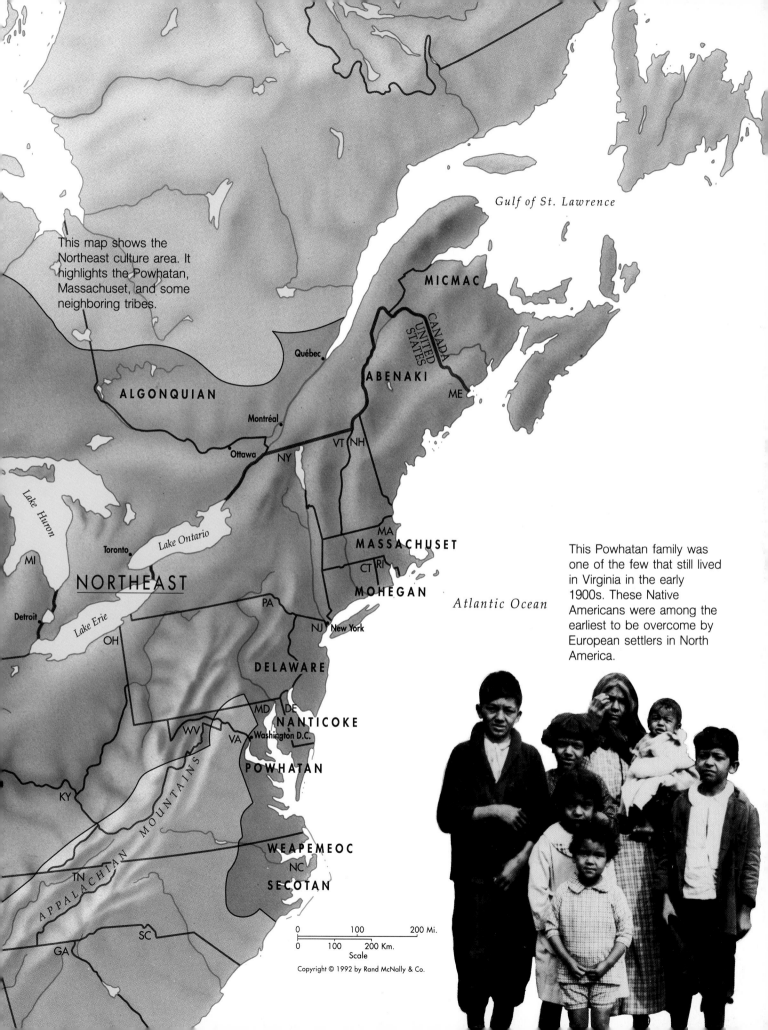

This map shows the Northeast culture area. It highlights the Powhatan, Massachuset, and some neighboring tribes.

Gulf of St. Lawrence

MICMAC

CANADA
UNITED STATES

Québec.

ABENAKI

ALGONQUIAN

ME

Montréal.

VT NH

Ottawa. NY

Lake Huron

Lake Ontario

Toronto.

MA

MI

MASSACHUSET

NORTHEAST

CT RI

MOHEGAN

Atlantic Ocean

PA

Detroit.

Lake Erie

OH

NJ New York

DELAWARE

This Powhatan family was one of the few that still lived in Virginia in the early 1900s. These Native Americans were among the earliest to be overcome by European settlers in North America.

MD DE

WV

NANTICOKE

VA Washington D.C.

POWHATAN

KY

WEAPEMEOC

NC

APPALACHIAN MOUNTAINS

TN

SECOTAN

SC

GA

0   100   200 Mi.
0   100   200 Km.
Scale

Copyright © 1992 by Rand McNally & Co.

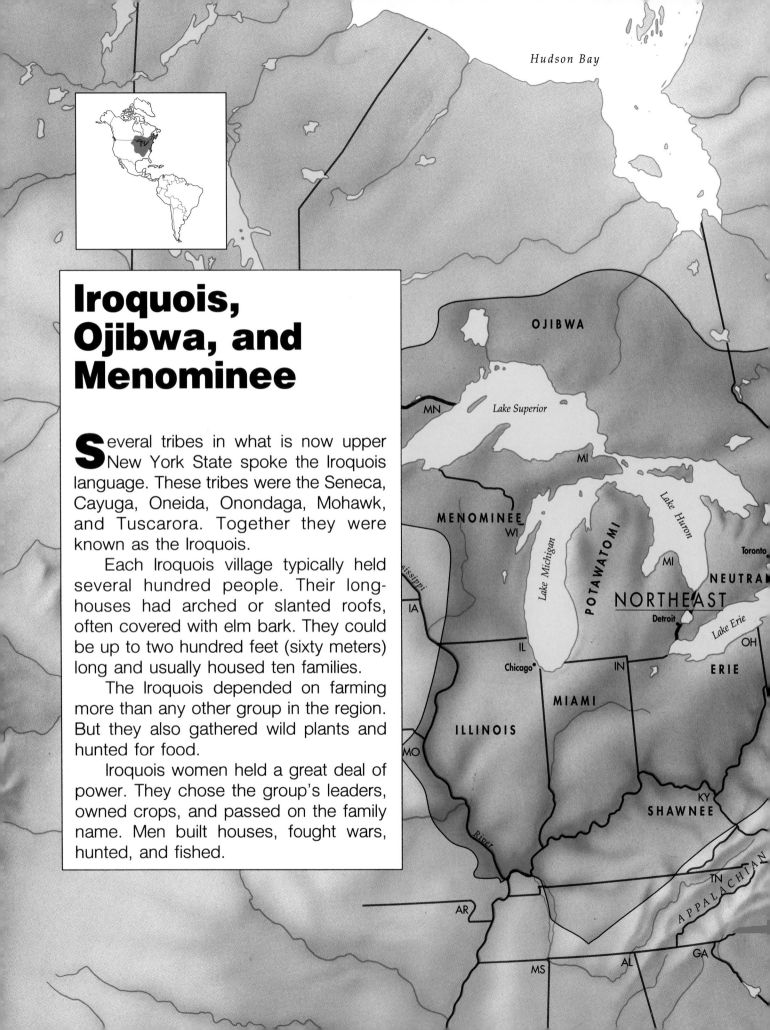

Iroquois, Ojibwa, and Menominee

Several tribes in what is now upper New York State spoke the Iroquois language. These tribes were the Seneca, Cayuga, Oneida, Onondaga, Mohawk, and Tuscarora. Together they were known as the Iroquois.

Each Iroquois village typically held several hundred people. Their longhouses had arched or slanted roofs, often covered with elm bark. They could be up to two hundred feet (sixty meters) long and usually housed ten families.

The Iroquois depended on farming more than any other group in the region. But they also gathered wild plants and hunted for food.

Iroquois women held a great deal of power. They chose the group's leaders, owned crops, and passed on the family name. Men built houses, fought wars, hunted, and fished.

Hudson Bay

OJIBWA

Lake Superior

MN

MI

MENOMINEE
WI

POTAWATOMI

Lake Michigan

Lake Huron

Toronto

MI

NEUTRA

NORTHEAST

Detroit

Lake Erie

OH

ERIE

IA

IL

Chicago

IN

MIAMI

MO

ILLINOIS

River

KY

SHAWNEE

TN

APPALACHIAN

AR

MS

AL

GA

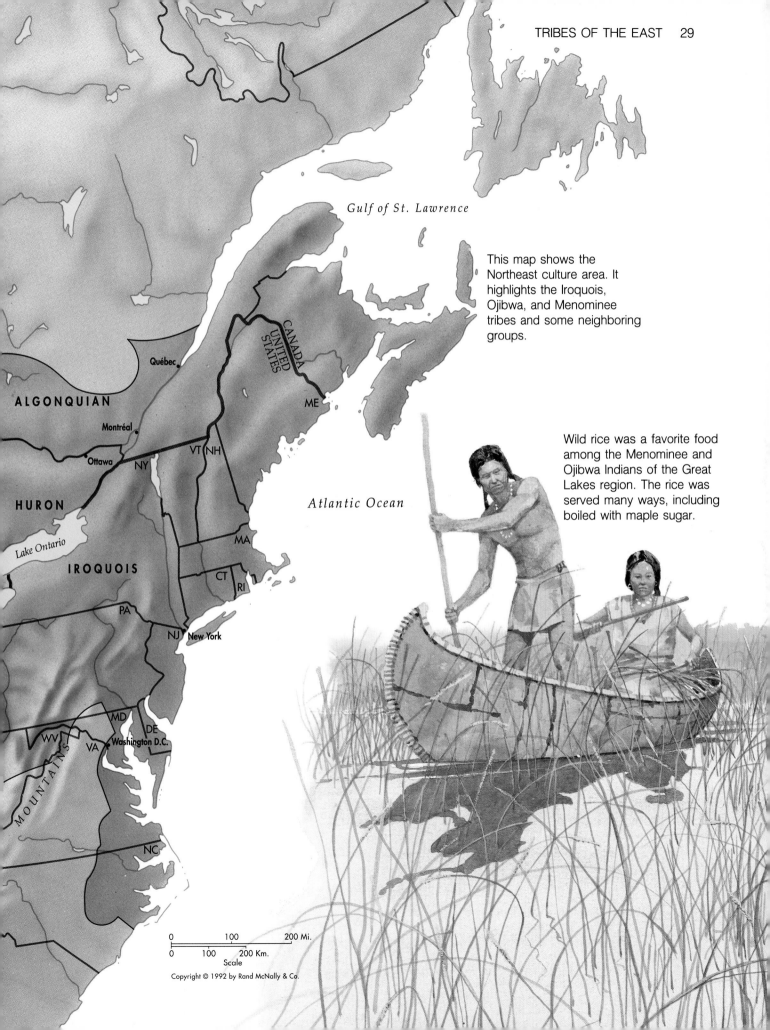

Gulf of St. Lawrence

This map shows the
Northeast culture area. It
highlights the Iroquois,
Ojibwa, and Menominee
tribes and some neighboring
groups.

Wild rice was a favorite food
among the Menominee and
Ojibwa Indians of the Great
Lakes region. The rice was
served many ways, including
boiled with maple sugar.

Québec

A L G O N Q U I A N

Montréal

Ottawa

NY

CANADA
UNITED
STATES

VT NH

ME

Atlantic Ocean

H U R O N

Lake Ontario

I R O Q U O I S

MA

CT
RI

PA

NJ   New York

MD

WV
DE

VA   Washington D.C.

M
O
U
N
T
A
I
N
S

NC

0   100   200 Mi.
0   100   200 Km.
Scale

Copyright © 1992 by Rand McNally & Co.

Sometime before 1600, the Iroquois-speaking groups united. The resulting group was the Iroquois League. It was the best organized and most powerful Indian group in the Northeast.

The Ojibwa, also known as the Chippewa, was a powerful group that lived in the northern Great Lakes region. Each Ojibwa tribe was made up of migrating bands, or groups that moved from one area to another. In the fall, family groups moved to the hunting grounds. Then in the summer, they gathered together again at the fishing grounds. These hunters grew small amounts of corn, pumpkin, and squash, but a more important food was the wild rice they gathered from the shores of the waterways.

Some Ojibwa groups lived differently. Those north of the Great Lakes lived as Subarctic tribes did and are considered part of the Subarctic culture area. To the west near the northern plains, some groups adopted the ways of the Plains Indians.

The Menominee Indians of northern Wisconsin lived a more settled life in permanent wigwam villages. A tall grass with rice-like seeds grew in large

The top of this Menominee lodge is folded back, showing a Medicine Dance taking place inside. The term "medicine" here means supernatural power, as well as the ability to cure the sick.

amounts along the nearby waterways. This "wild rice" served as a major source of food. The Menominee, as well as some Ojibwa, collected it by bending the plant stalks over their canoes. When they tapped the stalks, the grain fell into the boat's bottom.

This Mohawk woman is weaving in front of a birchbark canoe. The Mohawks were part of the powerful Iroquois League.

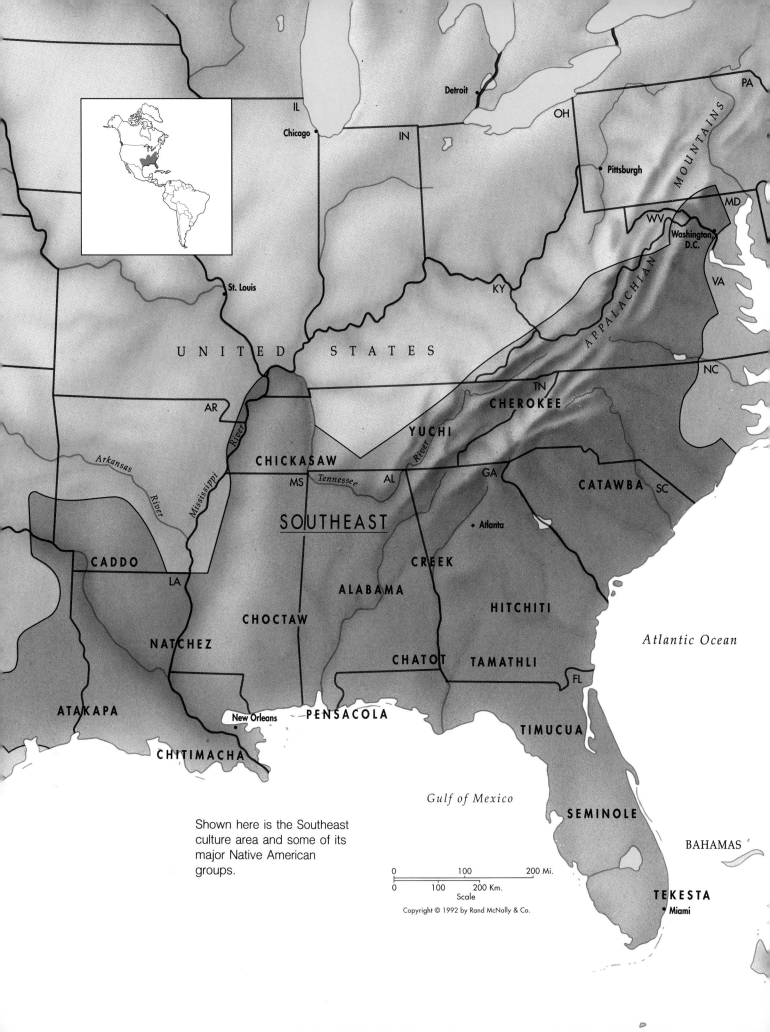

IL

Detroit

Chicago

PA

OH

IN

Pittsburgh

M
O
U
N
T
A
I
N
S

MD

St. Louis

KY

WV

Washington,
D.C.

U N I T E D   S T A T E S

VA

A
P
P
A
L
A
C
H
I
A
N

NC

TN

AR

CHEROKEE

River

Arkansas

YUCHI

River

Mississippi

CHICKASAW

MS

Tennessee

AL

GA

CATAWBA

SC

SOUTHEAST

Atlanta

CADDO

LA

CREEK

ALABAMA

HITCHITI

Atlantic Ocean

CHOCTAW

NATCHEZ

CHATOT

TAMATHLI

FL

ATAKAPA

New Orleans

PENSACOLA

TIMUCUA

CHITIMACHA

Gulf of Mexico

SEMINOLE

Shown here is the Southeast
culture area and some of its
major Native American
groups.

BAHAMAS

0   100   200 Mi.

0   100   200 Km.
Scale

TEKESTA

Miami

Copyright © 1992 by Rand McNally & Co.

Cherokee, Creek, and Seminole

The people of the Southeast culture area descended from the ancient Mound Builders. They developed what is thought to be the most advanced culture north of Mexico. The mild climate supported plenty of plants and wildlife and made conditions good for farming. Large-scale Indian settlements thrived.

The Cherokee were driven out of the Great Lakes area by other Native Americans. They settled in the Southeast along the Appalachian Mountains. With over two hundred villages, they were the largest and most powerful group in the region. Each village contained between thirty and sixty log houses. The Cherokee, like other Southeast groups, formed a union of "red towns" for war ceremonies and "white towns" for peace ceremonies.

For food, the Cherokee used bows and arrows to hunt large game, such as bear and deer. They used blow guns to kill squirrels, rabbits, and turkeys. Corn, beans, squash, and sunflowers grew well in the rich soil. The forests also held many plants that could be used for food.

The Creek lived in the flatlands of what is now Georgia and Alabama. The name *Creek* is an English name that was given to several different groups. The Muskogee, who lived in the northern

A small group of Seminoles remained in the Florida Everglades after the other American Indians were moved from the Southeast. This Seminole man spears a fish from his dugout canoe in about 1940.

A Creek man posed for this portrait about one hundred years ago.

lands, were called the Upper Creek. The Hitchiti and Alabama, in the southern region, were called the Lower Creek. Creek women did most of the farming. They grew beans, corn, and squash while the men hunted.

There were about fifty Creek villages. Each had a central plaza surrounded by houses made of wood and plaster. Within the plazas of many towns was a pyramid with a temple on top. These temple-pyramids looked a lot like the temple-pyramids of many Mexican groups. Some people believe that the Indians of the Southeast and those of Mexico had contact with one another.

The plaza was a gathering place for festivals. The most important was the midsummer Green Corn Festival. As a part of this festival, every crime except murder was forgiven. To prepare for the ceremony, villagers repaired and cleaned their buildings. Sometimes they even burned some of their possessions. The most important villagers fasted, then gathered for a great feast.

The name *Seminole* comes from a Creek word meaning "runaway." In the 1750s some Indians from Lower Creek towns moved southward. They joined the American Indians who lived in the Florida Everglades. By the 1800s, all these Native Americans began to be known as Seminoles. They built their villages along the rivers that ran through swamplands. They grew some plants, but mostly they hunted and fished for food. For shelter, they built simple, open dwellings out of poles and plants.

In the 1830s, most of the Cherokee, Creek, Seminole, Choctaw, and Chickasaw—later known as the Five Civilized Tribes—were forced from their homelands. The United States Army rounded them up and forced them to go to Indian Territory, which is now Oklahoma. They were treated very badly and many Indians died. The trip was so terrible that the Cherokee called the path they took the Trail of Tears. Only some small groups of Indians managed to stay in their homelands.

These Cherokee women were part of the small group that managed to stay in North Carolina while the others were moved to Oklahoma. The Great Smoky Mountains are still home to some Cherokee.

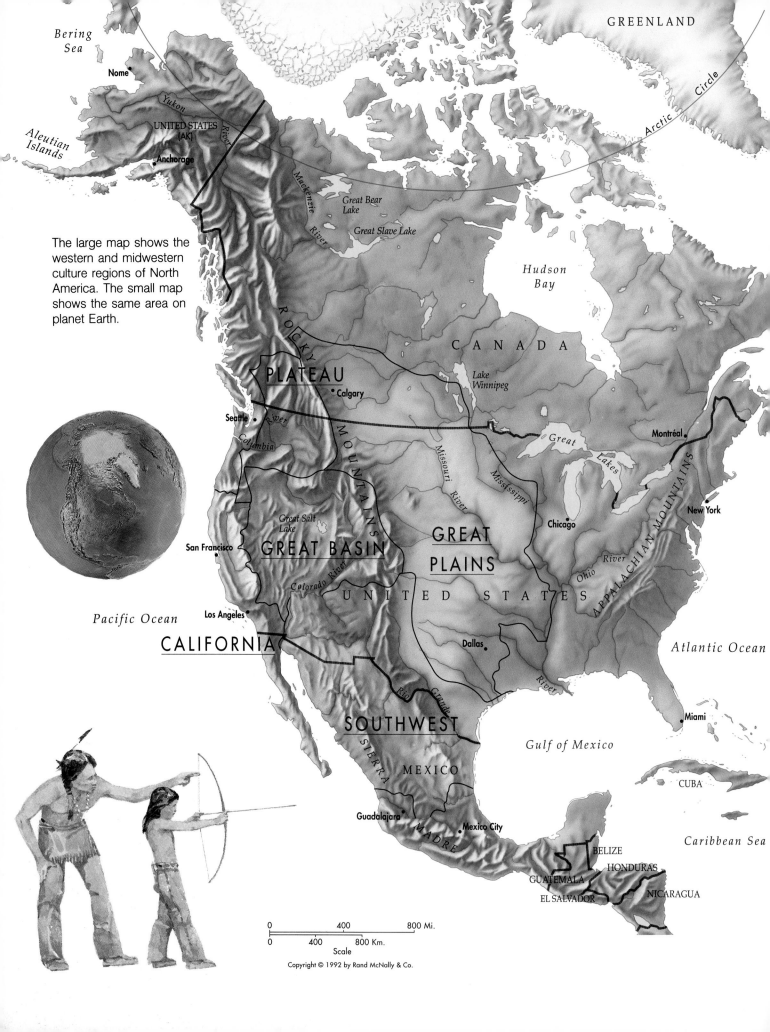

GREENLAND

Bering Sea

Nome •

Aleutian Islands

Yukon River

UNITED STATES (AK)

Anchorage •

Arctic Circle

Mackenzie River

Great Bear Lake

Great Slave Lake

Hudson Bay

C A N A D A

The large map shows the western and midwestern culture regions of North America. The small map shows the same area on planet Earth.

PLATEAU

Calgary •

Seattle •

Columbia River

Lake Winnipeg

Montréal •

Great Lakes

R O C K Y   M O U N T A I N S

Missouri River

Mississippi

Great Salt Lake

San Francisco •

GREAT BASIN

GREAT PLAINS

Chicago •

New York •

U N I T E D   S T A T E S

A P P A L A C H I A N   M O U N T A I N S

Colorado River

Ohio River

Los Angeles •

Pacific Ocean

CALIFORNIA

Dallas •

Atlantic Ocean

SOUTHWEST

Rio Grande

Miami •

Gulf of Mexico

River

S I E R R A

MEXICO

CUBA

Guadalajara •

Mexico City •

M A D R E

Caribbean Sea

BELIZE

HONDURAS

GUATEMALA

NICARAGUA

EL SALVADOR

0   400   800 Mi.
0   400   800 Km.
Scale

Copyright © 1992 by Rand McNally & Co.

Great Plains and Western Tribes

The Peoples of the Plains

The grasslands of the Great Plains extend from the Rocky Mountains to the Mississippi River and from southern Canada to the Gulf of Mexico. At one time, some sixty million bison, or buffalo, roamed in huge herds. Dozens of Native American groups depended on the bison to live. The Arapaho, Blackfeet, Cheyenne, Crow, Iowa, Pawnee, Dakota (better known as the Sioux), Plains Cree, and many more lived here. These were the peoples of the Plains.

The Plains Indians may be the Indians we picture when we think of Native Americans. But the culture we know did not come about until long after the Europeans arrived. In the 1500s, the Spanish explored far into the Americas. They left behind horses, which reshaped the way people lived.

Many Sioux groups lived on the Great Plains. Like other Plains hunters, the Sioux relied heavily on bison.

Horses made the Plains way of life much easier. Bison herds could be tracked over a much wider area. And, since horses could outrun bison, the bison could be killed more easily. This left more time for other activities.

The bison hunt was an important event for every village. When scouts warned of an approaching herd, villagers often set up traps. The traps forced the bison to the edge of a cliff or into an enclosed area.

Every part of the bison was used. The meat fed the tribe. The hide was used to cover portable homes called tepees. It was also used for shields, moccasins, and cup-shaped boats called *bullboats*. The animal's bones and horns became tools and cups.

Long before the horse, foraging nomads—people who moved from place to

Fellow members of a Hidatsa group look on as Dog Society warriors perform a ceremony. Members of the society did everything "backwards." For example, a Dog Society member who said "yes" really meant "no."

PLAINS CREE

•Calgary

BLACKFEET

•Regina

PLAINS OJIBWA

•Winnipeg

WA

CANADA
UNITED STATES

GROS VENTRE

ASSINIBOIN

ND

MN

Lake Super

OR

HIDATSA

MANDAN

WI

CROW

MT

SD

Minneapolis•

ID

WY

CHEYENNE

SIOUX

GREAT PLAINS

IA

CA

NV

NE

OMAHA

IOWA

IL

Chicago•

UT

PAWNEE

Missouri

ROCKY MOUNTAINS

Denver•

CO

MO

St. Louis•

ARAPAHO

KS MISSOURI

KANSA

River

Shown here is the Great
Plains culture area and
some of its major American
Indian groups.

NM

KIOWA

OK

OSAGE

AR

TN

TX

Arkansas

River

QUAPAW

MS

COMANCHE

WICHITA

Dallas•

LA

Mississippi River

Houston•

New Orleans•

UNITED STATES
MEXICO

Pacific Ocean

Gulf of Mexico

0		200		400 Mi.
0	200		400 Km.	

Scale

place in search of food—lived along the rivers of the Great Plains. They left the area around AD 1200. After that, the Pawnee, Arikara, Wichita, Mandan, and Hidatsa were probably the first to settle in the Plains. They were farmers who occupied the prairies along the Missouri River.

The Mandan, living in what is now North Dakota, were typical of these prairie farmers. They grew maize, squash, and sunflowers. They fished, and they hunted deer, bear, and other game. After the horse arrived, these farmers also spent part of every year on the plains hunting bison.

The Mandan lived in villages of up to one hundred *earth lodges*. An earth lodge began as a shallow round pit. Posts were placed around the outside to help form the walls. Other posts were used as roof supports. The Indians covered the inside posts with a thick layer of earth, then covered the roof posts with willow mats and earth. Usually between twenty and forty people shared each house.

Only a few non-farming Native American groups lived in the drier western Plains before 1500. One of these was the Blackfeet. Later many other tribes

Most people think of the horse-riding buffalo hunters of the Great Plains when they think of American Indians. Yet this way of life did not develop until the late 1600s. This was long after the Europeans and their horses arrived.

moved into the region including the Arapaho, Comanche, Cheyenne, Plains Cree, Plains Ojibwa, Kiowa, Sarcee, and Crow.

The Comanche settled in western Texas. They were one of the first groups to have horses. They kept huge herds of them and were expert trainers.

Trading between American Indian groups was common. People who didn't farm might exchange goods for the grain grown by farming people. The Cheyenne played an important role in the horse trade between southern tribes and Indians of the northern Plains. Items introduced by the Europeans, such as cloth, kettles, and guns, were thought to be so valuable that some groups would trade horses for them.

When white settlers came to the Great Plains, many Plains Indians began practicing the Ghost Dance. The dance was intended to bring back the Native American way of life. Here a group of Arapaho perform the Ghost Dance in 1893.

These Western Shoshone look for roots and seeds in the Great Basin. The desert provided a hard life for these Native Americans.

Shoshone, Ute, and Paiute

A vast, bowl-shaped desert area sits in the western part of the United States. Surrounded by the Rocky Mountains and the Sierra Nevada mountains, this region is known as the Great Basin. Its deepest point, Death Valley, marks the lowest and hottest spot in the Americas.

The Great Basin provided special challenges to the Native Americans who settled there. They traveled in small bands, searching the desert for the scarce food it could supply. This included seeds, roots, mice, gophers, snakes, lizards, and even grasshoppers. They lived in temporary cone-shaped dwellings made from poles covered with brush called *wickiups*.

Many Shoshone, Ute, and Paiute shared this way of life. Family groups would scatter in search of food in the summer. They would gather together again in the fall and winter for festivals and hunts. Groups rarely grew larger than fifty people.

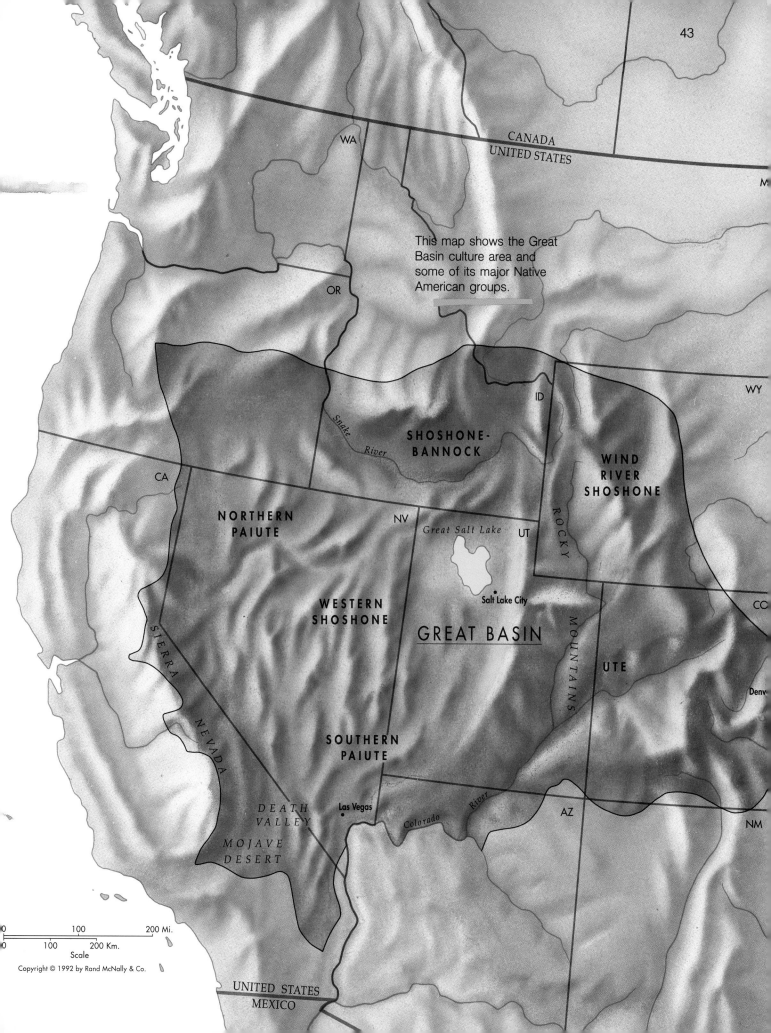

This map shows the Great Basin culture area and some of its major Native American groups.

CANADA
UNITED STATES

WA

OR

ID

WY

Snake

River

SHOSHONE-
BANNOCK

WIND
RIVER
SHOSHONE

CA

NORTHERN
PAIUTE

NV

Great Salt Lake

UT

ROCKY

S
I
E
R
R
A

N
E
V
A
D
A

WESTERN
SHOSHONE

Salt Lake City

GREAT BASIN

M
O
U
N
T
A
I
N
S

CO

UTE

Denv

SOUTHERN
PAIUTE

DEATH
VALLEY

Las Vegas

Colorado

River

AZ

NM

MOJAVE
DESERT

100   200 Mi.

100   200 Km.

Scale

UNITED STATES
MEXICO

There were two types of American Indian games: games of chance and games of skill. Here a group of Paiute men play a game in the 1870s.

The Northern Shoshone, who lived in what is now Wyoming and Idaho, hunted game in the mountain forests. They acquired horses in the late 1600s, as did the Wind River Shoshone. Then they began to live more like the Plains Indians, hunting bison and living in tepees.

The Ute lived in the area from western Colorado into northern New Mexico, northeastern Arizona, and Utah. In fact, the state of Utah takes its name from this tribe. The Ute gathered wild seeds and roots and hunted rabbit and antelope. They also fished in the rivers streaming west from the Rockies.

The Northern Paiute lived in parts of Oregon, Idaho, Nevada, Utah, and California. They hunted small animals and birds, and also ate pine nuts and cattails. For collecting and storing seeds, they made baskets.

Shown here is a Northern Shoshone village in 1870. These American Indians took on many ways of the Plains Indians when they acquired the horse in the 1600s.

The Southern Paiute lived in parts of Utah, Arizona, Nevada, and California. They supplemented their diet with corn and squash that they grew in small gardens.

This Ute household was photographed in Utah in the 1870s. The climate was hot, so little shelter was needed. The Great Basin groups were expert basket weavers.

The fate of the Klamath was the same as that of many American Indians. In the 1860s, they signed a treaty which turned their homeland into a reservation.

Klamath

Between the Cascade Range and the Rocky Mountains lies the Columbia Plateau. This region formed the Plateau culture area. It extended through parts of what is now the northwestern United States and southwestern Canada.

Grass and sagebrush cover the dry central part of the plateau. Thick forests of spruce, fir, pine, and cedar grow on the mountainsides. Native Americans in the grasslands ate wild onions, wild carrots, and the roots of the camas plant (a lily). At the edge of the forest they stalked elk, rabbit, or bear. But food was most plentiful near the rivers. The yearly runs of salmon, swimming upriver to lay their eggs, were an easy catch.

The Klamath settled the shores of marshes and lakes in what is now south-central Oregon. They lived in *pit houses*.

A pit house was made from a shallow hole in the ground with a log frame against its edges. The roof was made of saplings, reeds, and mud. These houses were cool in the summer and warm in the winter. The Klamath traveled the lakes and rivers of their homeland in dugout canoes.

Excellent with bow and arrow, the fierce Klamaths often raided the tribes in northern California. They took captives which they either kept as slaves or sold to other Indian groups.

After the introduction of the horse in the 1500s, many tribes of the eastern Plateau used horses to hunt bison. Their way of life became similar to that of the Plains Indians.

SHUSWAP

Calgary

PLATEAU

ROCKY

KUTENAI

Vancouver

WA

CANADA
UNITED STATES

ID

MT

Pacific Ocean

Seattle

COLUMBIA

SPOKANE

MOUNTAINS

This map shows
the Plateau culture
area and some of
its major American
Indian groups.

OR

RANGE

FLATHEAD

Columbia   *River*

Portland

TENINO

CAYUSE

River

NEZ PERCE

CASCADE

WY

Snake

KLAMATH

CA

MODOC

NV

UT

0	100	200 Mi.
0	100	200 Km.

Scale

The Chumash were the only Indians of North America to make boats from wooden planks. These boats allowed the Chumash to catch ocean fish, shellfish, and sea mammals such as seals.

Chumash

Many American Indian groups thrived in the mild weather and rich lands of what is now California. Wild plants and animals were so plentiful that these groups had no need for farming. They hunted deer, rabbit, and duck. They gathered berries, nuts, seeds, and roots. Their diet even included insects such as caterpillars and grasshoppers.

The acorn was one of the region's most important foods. The Indians dried the kernels in the sun and pounded them into a powder. Then they washed the powder to remove the bitter taste. The result was a flour that was used in soup or baked into bread. Coastal Indians added fish and other seafood to their diets.

One of these coastal groups was the Chumash. Many Indians built rafts or dugout canoes for water travel, but the Chumash were the only North American Indians to build boats from wooden planks. They split cedar logs, then bound them together with plant fibers. They sealed the gaps between the planks with asphalt. The boats were 25 feet long (7.6 meters) and were probably used for traveling between offshore islands as well as for fishing.

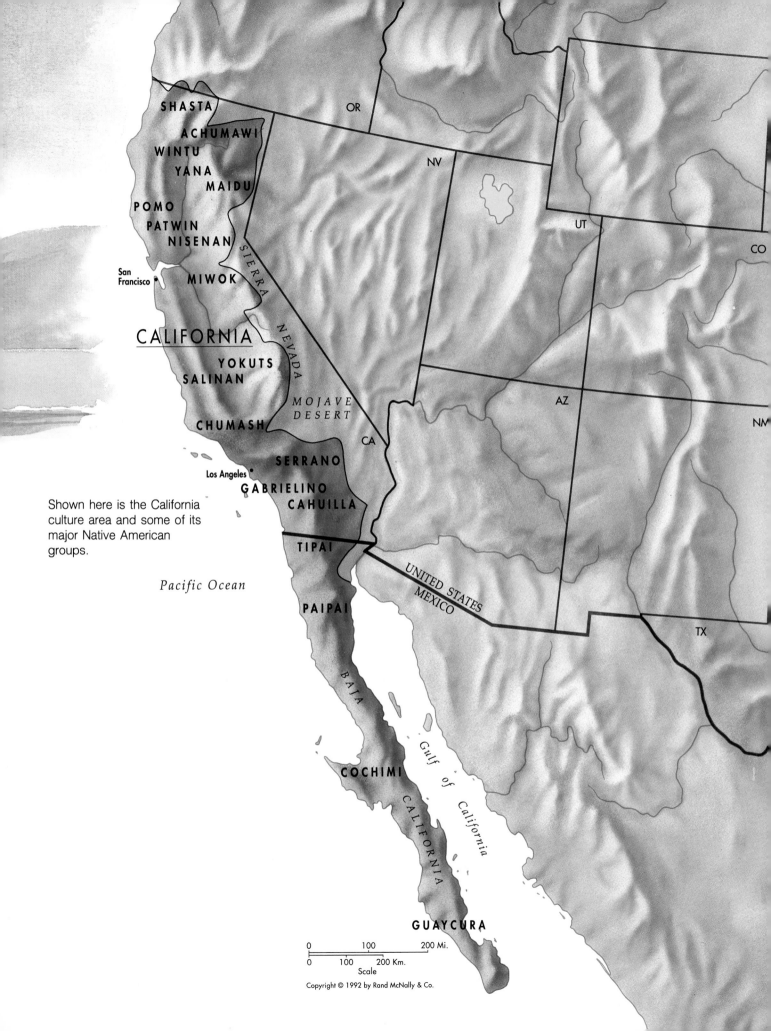

SHASTA

ACHUMAWI

WINTU

YANA

MAIDU

POMO

PATWIN

NISENAN

San Francisco

MIWOK

CALIFORNIA

YOKUTS

SALINAN

SIERRA NEVADA

MOJAVE DESERT

CHUMASH

CA

SERRANO

Los Angeles

GABRIELINO

CAHUILLA

TIPAI

Shown here is the California culture area and some of its major Native American groups.

Pacific Ocean

PAIPAI

UNITED STATES
MEXICO

BAJA

COCHIMI

CALIFORNIA

Gulf of California

OR

NV

UT

CO

AZ

NM

TX

GUAYCURA

| 0 | 100 | 200 Mi. |
| 0 | 100 | 200 Km. |

Scale

Copyright © 1992 by Rand McNally & Co.

Apache, Navajo, and Hopi

A Navajo man tends his sheep in Monument Valley, Arizona. Today, the Navajo are the largest North American Indian group.

Rugged lands make up the Southwest culture area. Tribes from this area all lived very differently. Some, like the Apache and Navajo, moved from place to place as they hunted and gathered food. Others, like the Hopi, were desert farmers.

The most common Apache home was the *wickiup*, a domed or cone-shaped hut. It was made from a wooden frame covered with grass or brush. In general, the Apache ate whatever game, fruits and vegetables they could find. Some groups also farmed or hunted bison.

The Navajo became farmers after contact with the Hopi in the 1700s. They raised corn, beans, squash, and melons. They also raided other tribes and European settlements for food.

Navajos were expert silversmiths and weavers. Behind these Navajos is a hogan, a typical Navajo home.

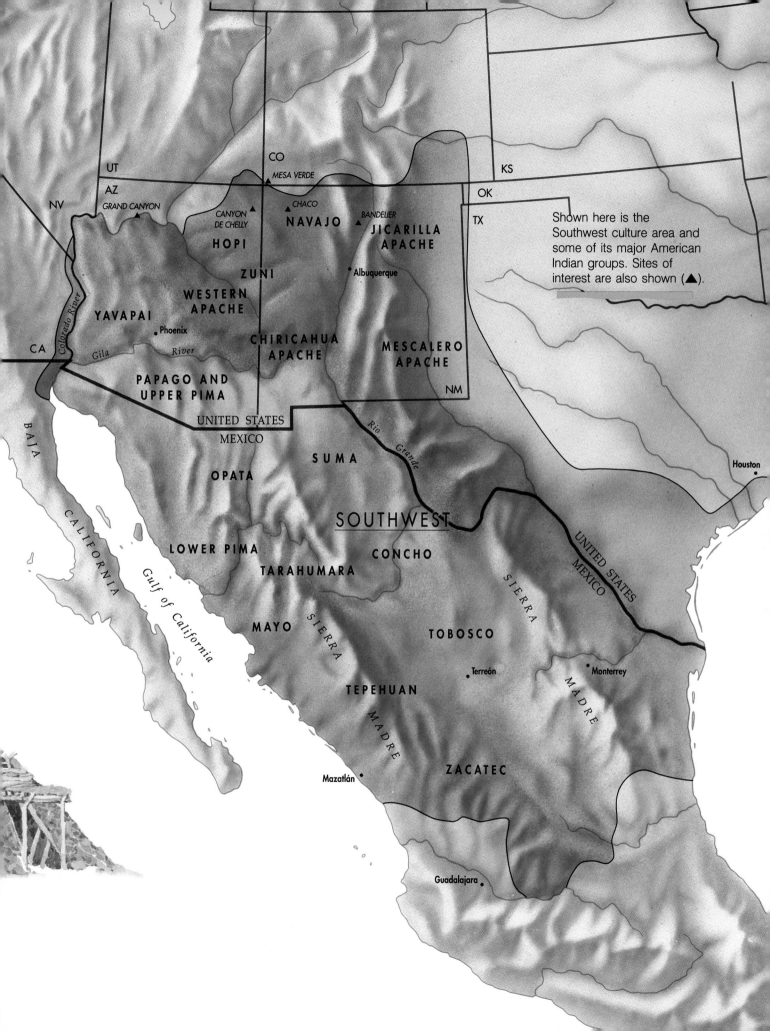

UT

CO

KS

NV

AZ

OK

TX

MESA VERDE

GRAND CANYON

CHACO

BANDELIER

CANYON
DE CHELLY

NAVAJO

JICARILLA
APACHE

Shown here is the
Southwest culture area and
some of its major American
Indian groups. Sites of
interest are also shown (▲).

HOPI

ZUNI

• Albuquerque

WESTERN
APACHE

YAVAPAI

CHIRICAHUA
APACHE

MESCALERO
APACHE

CA

• Phoenix

Colorado River

Gila   River

PAPAGO AND
UPPER PIMA

NM

UNITED STATES
MEXICO

SUMA

Rio Grande

Houston •

OPATA

BAJA

SOUTHWEST

UNITED STATES
MEXICO

CALIFORNIA

LOWER PIMA

CONCHO

SIERRA

TARAHUMARA

Gulf of California

MAYO

SIERRA

TOBOSCO

MADRE

Terreón •

• Monterrey

MADRE

TEPEHUAN

Mazatlán •

ZACATEC

Guadalajara •

52

Most Apaches never did settle and become farmers like other American Indians in the Southwest. Here a group of young Apache men pose with bows and arrows.

Their homes were cone-shaped *hogans* made of log-and-stick frames covered with earth. Today, the Navajo is the largest group of Native Americans in the United States.

The Hopi are thought to be descendants of the Anasazi, who lived in the area hundreds of years earlier. Like the Anasazi, they built large pueblos. These buildings had many levels and were made from sun-dried bricks of mud and straw called adobe. Towns were usually placed atop high mesas—flat-topped hills or mountains with cliff-like sides.

The Hopi were very successful as farmers in the hot, dry climate. They learned to plant crops near underground springs or at the base of the mesas, where the crops could catch the runoff from any rainfall.

Hopis believed that supernatural beings called *kachinas* lived in the San Francisco Mountains. Men wore kachina masks during special ceremonies. Hopi parents carved kachina dolls for their children.

The Hopi men shown here wear masks to take on the spirits of *kachinas*. Other members of the group watch from atop pueblos.

These young Apaches were photographed playing a game in Arizona in 1899.

New Orleans

MEXICO

Gulf of Mexico

Miami

Atlantic Ocean

CUBA

Caribbean Sea

The large map shows some of the culture areas of Central and South America. The small map shows about the same area on planet Earth.

Guadalajara

Mexico City

MESOAMERICA

BELIZE

GUATEMALA

EL SALVADOR

COSTA RICA

PANAMA

HONDURAS

NICARAGUA

CARIBBEAN

Caracas

VENEZUELA

GUYANA

SURINAME

FRENCH GUIANA

COLOMBIA

Santa Fe de Bogotá

Equator

Amazon River

ECUADOR

Pacific Ocean

AMAZONIA

BRAZIL

PERU

Lima

ANDES

São Paulo

BOLIVIA

PARAGUAY

MOUNTAINS

ARGENTINA

URUGUAY

Santiago

Buenos Aires

SOUTHERN

CHILE

SOUTH

AMERICA

0   400   800 Mi.

0   400   800 Km.

Scale

Copyright © 1992 by Rand McNally & Co.

This photograph was taken in about 1900 at Monte Albán in Oaxaca, Mexico. The stone carvings were made by Zapotecs many centuries before.

Central and South American Peoples

Zapotec

Ancestors of the modern Zapotec created one of the earliest civilizations of Mexico. Their culture began before both the Aztec and the Maya cultures. By about 500 BC, the Zapotec had built a huge city surrounded by farms. Their ceremonial center at Monte Albán has the oldest hieroglyphics, or picture-based writing, ever found in the Americas. The Zapotec also built an observatory for studying astronomy. The development of the calendar probably began here.

Between AD 300 and 900, more than 60,000 people lived in Monte Albán. The city had stone pyramids, palaces, and painted tombs. Monte Albán became less important after AD 800, but Zapotec culture thrived in small towns. Around 1300, some Zapotec moved south and founded another city at Mitla.

The Zapotec now live in the Mexican state of Oaxaca. They are known for their beautiful weaving and sculpture. Today, over 400,000 people speak the Zapotec language.

Zapotec women and children pose here in Oaxaca around 1900. Zapotecs have lived in this part of Mexico for about two thousand years.

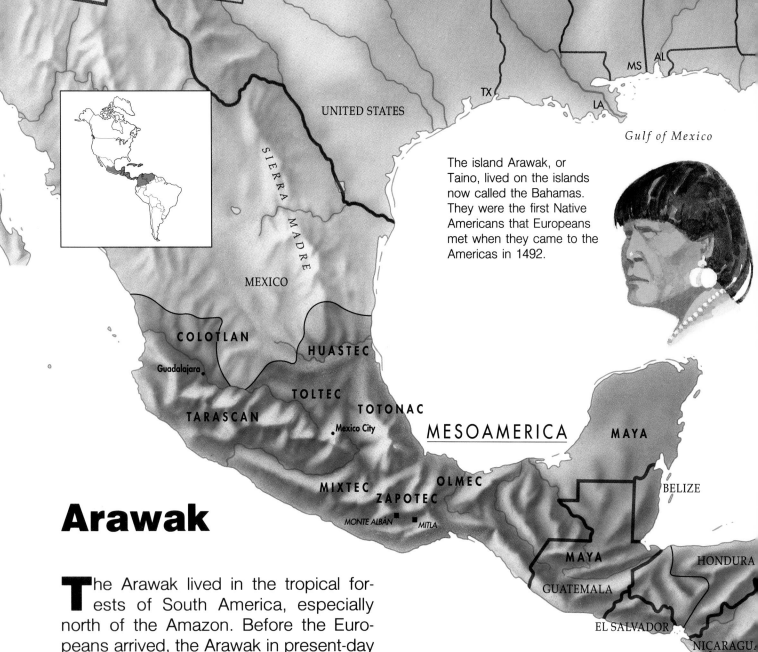

The island Arawak, or Taino, lived on the islands now called the Bahamas. They were the first Native Americans that Europeans met when they came to the Americas in 1492.

UNITED STATES

Gulf of Mexico

SIERRA MADRE

MEXICO

COLOTLAN

Guadalajara

HUASTEC

TOLTEC

TARASCAN

TOTONAC

Mexico City

MESOAMERICA

MIXTEC

OLMEC

ZAPOTEC

MONTE ALBÁN   MITLA

MAYA

BELIZE

MAYA

HONDURA

GUATEMALA

EL SALVADOR

NICARAGUA

TX   LA

MS   AL

Arawak

The Arawak lived in the tropical forests of South America, especially north of the Amazon. Before the Europeans arrived, the Arawak in present-day Guyana, Suriname, and Brazil gathered in large communities.

One Arawak group moved north, settling the islands of the Caribbean. These island Arawak were known as the Taino. The warm, wet climate of the Caribbean helped the Taino farm. Their crops included manioc roots, peanuts, and sweet potatoes. They also grew cotton which they used to make clothing and the hammocks in which they slept. The Taino traveled as far away as Mexico and Florida in their dugout canoes. There they traded goods with other tribes.

The Taino were driven from the eastern islands by the Carib Indians. When Christopher Columbus arrived in the Bahama Islands in 1492, the Taino were there to greet him. The Taino were the first Native Americans that Columbus met. Because Columbus thought he had reached India, he called these people "Indians."

Today, the Arawak live mainly in the forests of northeastern Brazil in groups of fewer than two hundred people. Often, their settlements consist of a single building in which everyone lives.

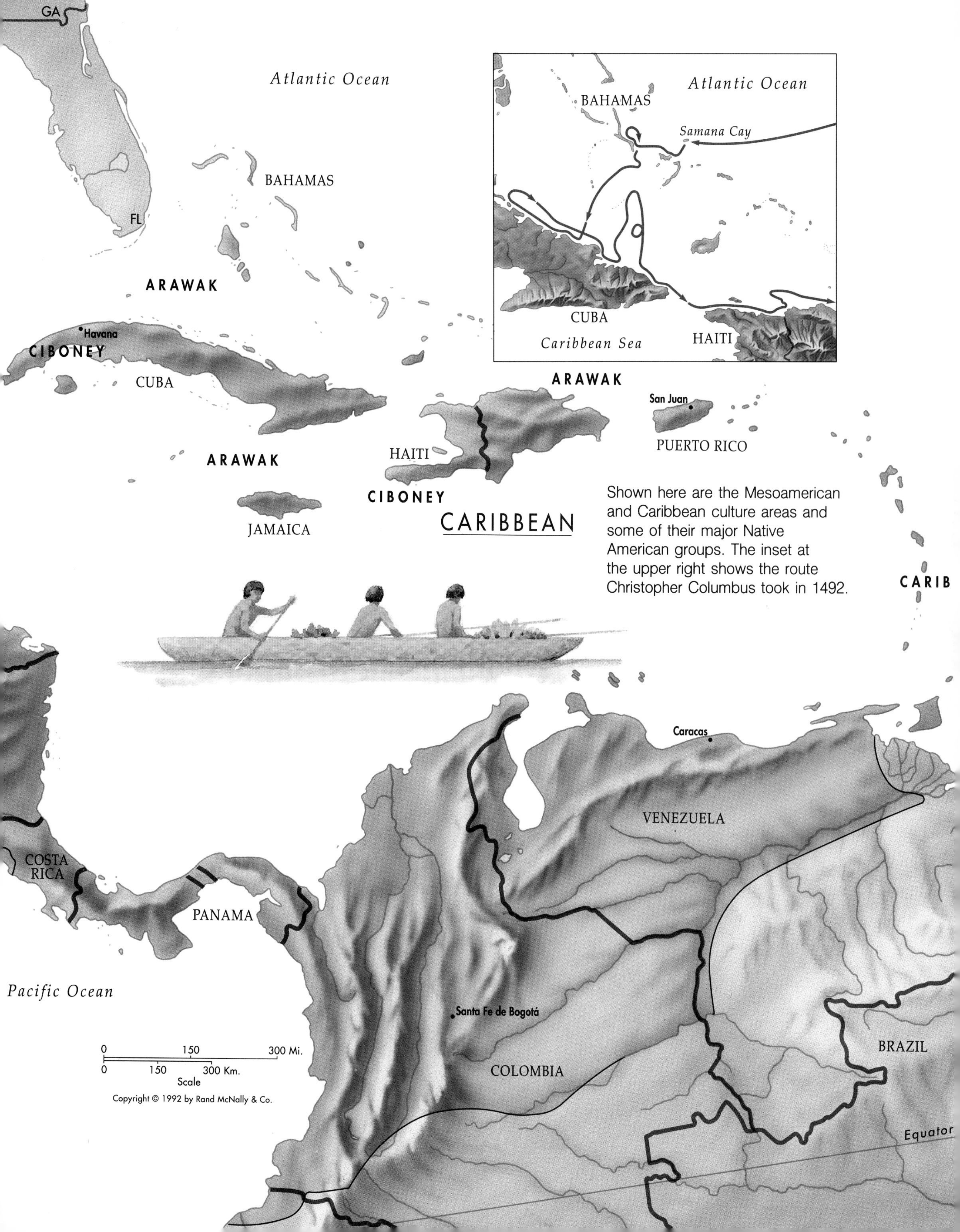
GA
FL
Atlantic Ocean
BAHAMAS
ARAWAK
Havana
CIBONEY
CUBA
ARAWAK
JAMAICA
HAITI
CIBONEY
CARIBBEAN
ARAWAK
San Juan
PUERTO RICO
CARIB
BAHAMAS
Atlantic Ocean
Samana Cay
CUBA
Caribbean Sea
HAITI
Caracas
VENEZUELA
COSTA RICA
PANAMA
Pacific Ocean
Santa Fe de Bogotá
COLOMBIA
BRAZIL
Equator
0 150 300 Mi.
0 150 300 Km.
Scale
Copyright © 1992 by Rand McNally & Co.

Shown here are the Mesoamerican and Caribbean culture areas and some of their major Native American groups. The inset at the upper right shows the route Christopher Columbus took in 1492.

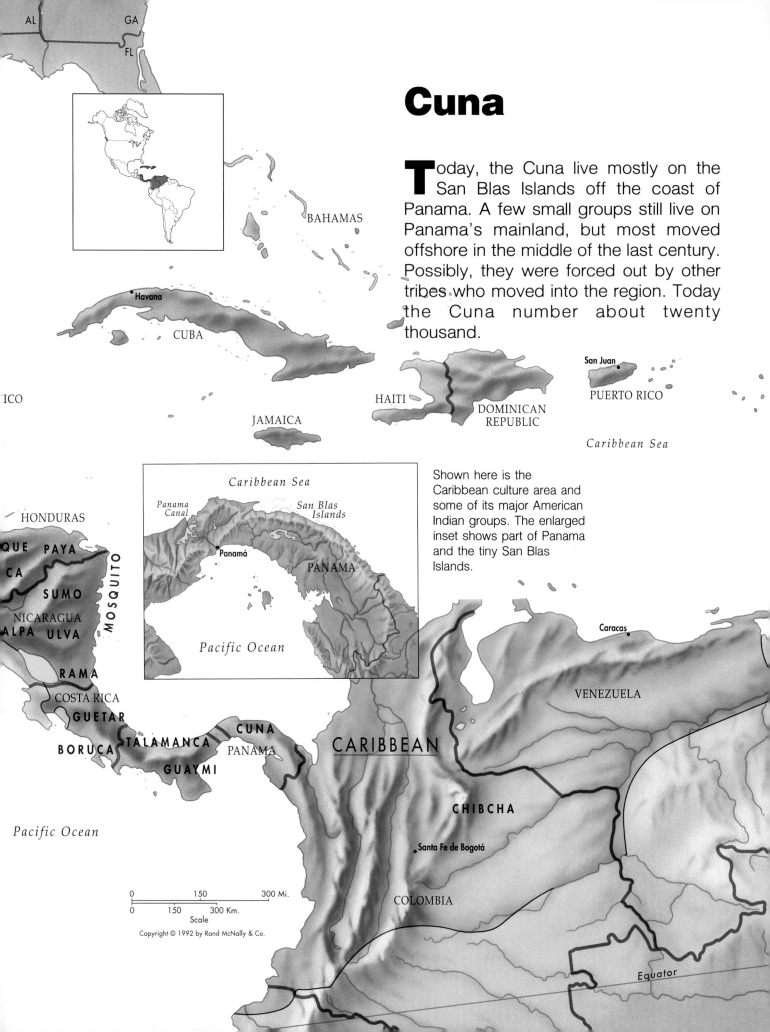

Cuna

Today, the Cuna live mostly on the San Blas Islands off the coast of Panama. A few small groups still live on Panama's mainland, but most moved offshore in the middle of the last century. Possibly, they were forced out by other tribes who moved into the region. Today the Cuna number about twenty thousand.

Shown here is the Caribbean culture area and some of its major American Indian groups. The enlarged inset shows part of Panama and the tiny San Blas Islands.

AL
GA
FL

BAHAMAS

Havana
CUBA

ICO

HAITI
DOMINICAN
REPUBLIC

San Juan
PUERTO RICO

JAMAICA

Caribbean Sea

Caribbean Sea

Panama Canal

San Blas Islands

Panamá

PANAMA

Pacific Ocean

HONDURAS

QUE   PAYA

CA

SUMO

NICARAGUA

ALPA   ULVA

M O S Q U I T O

RAMA

COSTA RICA

GUETAR

BORUCA   TALAMANCA   CUNA

GUAYMI   PANAMA

Pacific Ocean

CARIBBEAN

Caracas

VENEZUELA

CHIBCHA

Santa Fe de Bogotá

COLOMBIA

Equator

| 0 | 150 | 300 Mi. |
| 0 | 150 | 300 Km. |

Scale

The Cuna live in small villages. While most of their food comes from farming, they also hunt and fish the rich waters around the islands. In fact the native word *Panama* means "an abundance of fish." Corn, beans, squash, rice, and citrus fruits are their most important crops.

In Cuna religion, the souls of the dead must pass through eight layers of an underworld and then eight layers of heaven. *Shamans*, or spiritual guides, lead the souls on their journey.

The Cuna still speak the language of the Chibcha. Before the arrival of Europeans, the Chibcha spread throughout what is now Colombia. They lived in cities of several thousand people. The capital of modern Colombia, Bogotá, was the site of the main Chibcha ceremonial center. The Chibcha's society was nearly as complex as the Inca society in Peru. In the 1530's the Spanish began taking control of the area. The Chibcha, like the Inca, were defeated.

Atlantic Ocean

Cuna farmers grow most of the food they need, and the Caribbean waters provide plenty of fish. The reverse-appliqué blouses made by Cuna women, called *molas*, are known throughout the world.

GUYANA

SURINAME

BRAZIL

This map shows the Amazon culture area, or Amazonia, and some of its Native American groups.

Deep in the Amazon rain forest of Brazil and Venezuela, tribes like the Yanomami have had little contact with the modern world.

Caracas

VENEZUELA

CARIB

Atlantic Ocean

GUYANA

ARAWAK

ANAMA

FRENCH GUIANA

Santa Fe de Bogotá

SURINAME

COLOMBIA

YANOMAMI

WAIWAI

0   300   600 Mi.

0   300   600 Km.

Scale

Copyright © 1992 by Rand McNally & Co.

Equator

BARAUÁNA

Amazon

River

AMAZONIA

MAUÉ

TEMBÉ

ANDES

MONTANA

BRAZIL

Lima

MOUNTAINS

NAMBIKUARA

BOLIVIA

CHIQUITO

Brasília

Yanomami

Native Americans have lived in South America for at least ten thousand years. But no one knows how long they have lived in the rain forest of the Amazon River basin. This is because few non-natives ventured into the thick forests until the 1950s. Amazon Indians have had little contact with outsiders.

Hundreds of groups live in this rain forest. While the groups differ from one another in many ways, they have many things in common. The groups live in small communities, and most get food by hunting, fishing, and gathering plants, depending on the season.

The Yanomami is the largest tribe in the Americas that has kept its traditional ways. Because they have not been disturbed by outsiders, they have not had to change. They live deep in the forests of northwestern Brazil and southern Venezuela. In 1991 both countries set up areas of protected land for use by the Yanomami. This land covers more than

30,000 square miles (78,000 square kilometers).

The tribe's language does not seem to be related to the languages spoken by other South American groups. Because outsiders have had so little contact with the Yanomami, no one is sure of their number. Estimates vary from ten thousand to forty thousand.

Yanomami men frequently fight one another, and villages break up when relatives become enemies. Neighboring villages often raid one another. For this reason, enemy villages are so far apart that it may take days to walk between them. However, villages on friendly terms may lie within just a few hundred feet of each other.

The Yanomami grow bananas and plantains. They also gather palm fruit and hunt for additional food.

Mapuche women weave fabrics on a Chilean reservation.

Mapuche

The Araucanians are a group of Indians who speak related languages. They live in the Andes Mountains of southern South America. Once a widespread group of farmers and herders, today their numbers are much smaller. The Mapuche make up the largest group of Araucanian-speaking people. They live in the central valley of Chile.

Since the end of the last century, the Mapuche have lived on land set aside by the government of Chile. About 300,000 Mapuche live on these reservations today. They are the largest Native American group in modern South America. Those who don't live on the reservations have taken jobs in the cities of Chile and Argentina.

The Mapuche resisted when the Inca tried to expand southward into their lands. They are also known for their three-century struggle with the Spanish and, later, Chilean armies. These con-flicts forced them to change their traditional ways. Distant villages began to work together, and Mapuche warriors learned to use horses.

Farming remains the main activity of the Mapuche. They grow corn, potatoes, beans, squash, chili peppers, and other vegetables. In the past, when the men fought battles with other Mapuche groups or with the Spanish, the women cared for the crops. Today, though, men usually work the farms while the women tend to smaller vegetable gardens.

Fishing and hunting were also important to the Mapuche's ancient way of life. They used llamas to help them carry goods. At one time a person's wealth was measured by the number of llamas he owned. Today the llama herds have been replaced by horses, sheep, cattle, and other farm and ranch animals.

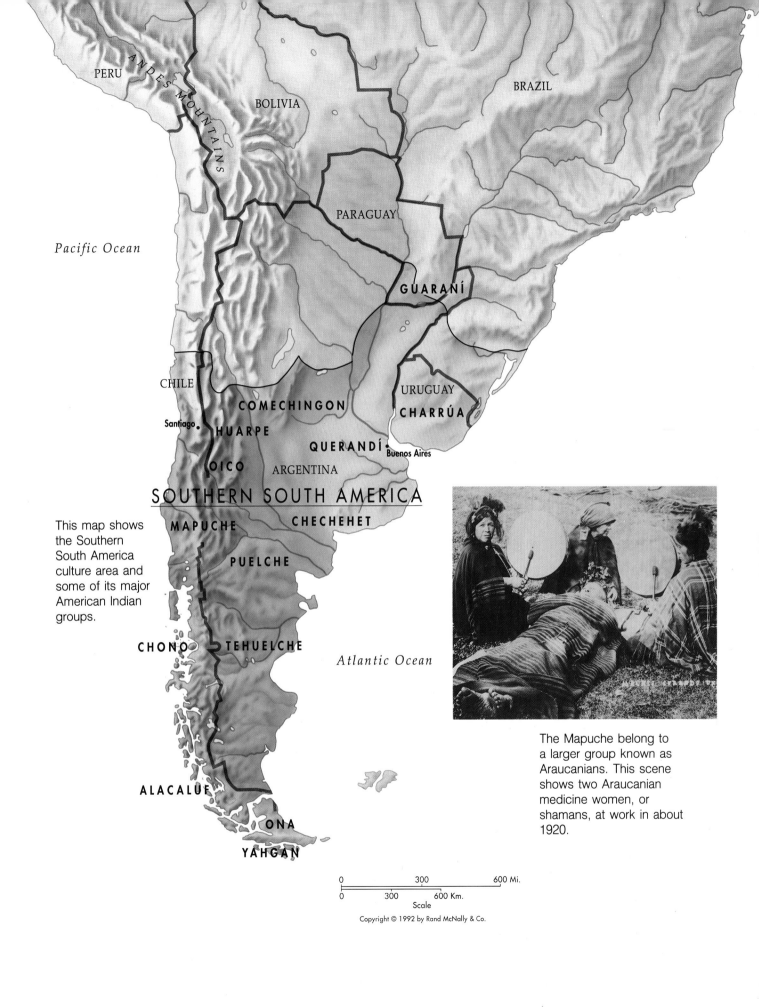

PERU

BRAZIL

BOLIVIA

ANDES MOUNTAINS

Pacific Ocean

PARAGUAY

GUARANÍ

CHILE

URUGUAY

COMECHINGON

CHARRÚA

Santiago •

HUARPE

QUERANDÍ
• Buenos Aires

OICO

ARGENTINA

SOUTHERN SOUTH AMERICA

This map shows
the Southern
South America
culture area and
some of its major
American Indian
groups.

MAPUCHE

CHECHEHET

PUELCHE

CHONO

TEHUELCHE

Atlantic Ocean

ALACALUF

ONA

YAHGAN

The Mapuche belong to
a larger group known as
Araucanians. This scene
shows two Araucanian
medicine women, or
shamans, at work in about
1920.

0   300   600 Mi.
0   300   600 Km.
Scale

Copyright © 1992 by Rand McNally & Co.

Index